VIEWS · FROM · A · TUSCAN · VINEYARD

For all those who have helped us with this book

Sir Harold Acton
Adam Alvarez
Albiera Antinori
Marchese Piero Antinori
Andrew Best
Giorgio Bianchi
Edgar and Charlotte de Bresson
Olietta Budini-Gattai
Marchese Carlo Citterio
Ursula Creagh
Contessa Marinetta di Frassineto
Marchese Leonardo de' Frescobaldi
Iain Fraser
Conte and Contessa Guicciardini
Bernard Higton
Susan Holt
Jane Kramer
Sandra Monassei
The Mariotti family
John Meis
Susan Mitchell
Sheila More
Ludovico de Santillana
Bette Ann Scavetta
Richard Seaver
Steven Spurrier
William and Rosemary Righter
David Rundle
Lele Vitali
Colin Webb

VIEWS · FROM · A · TUSCAN · VINEYARD

PHOTOGRAPHED BY CAREY MORE ◊ WRITTEN BY JULIAN MORE

PAVILION
MICHAEL JOSEPH

First published in Great Britain in 1987
by Pavilion Books Ltd,
196 Shaftesbury Avenue, London WC2H 8JL
in association with Michael Joseph Limited,
27 Wrights Lane, London W8 5TZ

Designed by Bernard Higton

British Library in Cataloguing Publication Data

More, Julian
    Views from a Tuscan vineyard.
    1. Tuscany (Italy) – Description and travel
    I. Title   II. More, Carey
    914.5'504928   DG734.2

    ISBN 1-85145-045-9

Photoset by Rowland Phototypesetting Limited,
Bury St Edmunds, Suffolk

Colour separation by CLG, Verona
Printed and bound in Italy by Arnoldo Mondadori

CONTENTS

INTRODUCTION

Views From A Tuscan Vineyard is a jigsaw of the past, the present, coincidence and luck. It was as if I were drawn from point to point for my photographs, by a force stronger than me. I was shown Tuscany by the people whose paths I crossed.

The coincidences started at the National Theatre, London, at the launch of my Photographic Exhibition in 1985. Adam, a friend I had not encountered for eleven years, appeared out of the blue. Seeing him reminded me of a summer spent with him and his family in Tuscany when I was barely sixteen. I was already preparing this book, and Adam's knowledge, I knew, would be helpful. We made instant plans.

A month later I found myself seated at a bar, in the heat of a Tuscan September night, with another old school-friend Sue, now a successful textile designer in Florence.

We were meeting Adam – my newly acquired guide, map reader, and interpreter. Much Chianti and pasta were demolished on a crowded terrace in the heart of Florence to celebrate our reunion – it was exhilarating to be with such good old friends at the start of my work.

Early next morning, in the already burning heat, we headed from Florence south to Radda in Chianti.

Greeted at Spanda by Ursula, Adam's mother, I was given a tour of the beautiful crumbling old farmhouse. A strong sense of familiarity swept over me, as I reacquainted myself with the faded mural of the family, the large anvil-shaped fireplace, and long trestle table round which teenagers, children, house guests, cats and dogs still gathered for riotous pasta lunches. House rules remained the same – no showers, no water wastage, no flushing of loos. Big signs were pinned up all over the house: the summer drought was still on.

September was a difficult month to take photographs, because of the blinding heat which builds up from ten o'clock onwards, and the dust that fills the air, casting a bluish haze everywhere. Dreams of capturing the translucent quality of my favourite Renaissance paintings vanished into thick air. Summer in Tuscany is above all for festivals. Of wine, of saints, of music. We frequented many – an outdoor violin concert at San Giusto a Rentennano, a harpsichord recital at Badia a Coltibuono, the wine *festa* at Radda. I immersed myself in Tuscan vitality and festivity. The joy of life is very strong there.

Winter was more gruelling. Staying in an unheated sixth floor apartment with Sue, I discovered Florence at

VITALI TOWER

MONTE ARGENTARIO

twenty degrees below – one small gas stove gallantly trying to warm us through. Leaving at dawn to catch the first light made for long days in the freezing open air. Once, exhausted by the cold, I had to pull over to the side of the road to rest. I slept for a good hour, and was later told what a risk I had taken: the Florence sex murderer 'Il Mostro' (The Monster) was still on the loose.

But luck was in store for me. It snowed, which is fairly rare in Tuscany. I had travelled down to Bagno Vignoni in the Val d'Orcia to take shots of the Roman Baths. After a robust, warming meal of homemade pasta, veal, *vin santo*

and almond biscuits in Pienza, I fell asleep in a room overlooking the Baths. Awoken by my alarm, I opened the shutters to see thick snowflakes covering the roofs and steam rising from the hot mineral waters. It was a magical moment. By mid-morning the snow had gone, replaced by sludgy mud.

Springtime was my favourite season. Lush green grass, flowers in abundance, warm temperatures, skies dramatically changeable – the sproutings of a new year. The air was clear and fresh. Vividly, the striking changes of Tuscany would inspire me – from wild, rolling prairie to intimate, bosky meadow.

In late spring and early summer, my father and I stayed in a tower at Radda in Chianti. We were in luck with both the view over the vineyard towards the village of Radda, and with our new-found friends the Vitalis who owned the tower. Many evenings were spent in their nearby house, sharing wine, food, and ideas for new explorations.

Passionate appreciation of Tuscany and its history was a sentiment we found everywhere. From top winemaker to local farmer – everyone expressed a love of their country that was totally infectious. As a visitor, I hope I have done them justice.

Carey More
Paris 1986

BAGNO VIGNONI

'I believe there is much happiness in people who are born where good wines are to be found,' said Leonardo da Vinci. But what of these times of poisoned wine scandal? Had that maverick Tuscan prophet for once got the future wrong? Would terrorist-terrified Americans desert the Piazza della Signoria and the bongo drums go silent outside the Uffizi? Would psychiatric wards empty of culture-shocked ladies from Woomera and Dayton, Ohio, their madness a conviction that Donatello is an ice cream and Gelato a sculptor? And Florence be left to the Florentines?

Not at all. At the cafés of the Via Tornabuoni, that lady from Dayton, Ohio, is still ordering her *donatello con fragole*. And in high summer the village bar of Radda, in the heart of Chiantishire, still echoes with the bray of the English home counties. Seldom is heard a word of Italian, though the Tuscans produced the first Italian dictionary.

My own love of Tuscany dates from a bone-shattering motorcycle ride to Florence from Perugia, where I had been learning Italian at the University for Foreigners. 1949 was not a good year for roads. Much of the bumpy, up-and-down trip in hallucinatory sunshine took us along 8th Army tank tracks, through hill villages so untouched by time their inhabitants mistook us for stragglers from the Liberation. We were royally treated. Wine flowed, toasts were drunk. The wine took the top of my mouth off, but in those happy circumstances it tasted like nectar.

Later, I wrote a song called 'Chianti' (it rhymes with Dante, though my influence at that time was another poet – Cole Porter). It appeared in my first musical *Grab Me A Gondola*, and in spite of that number the show was a hit. Quite why the chorus was singing the praises of Chianti in Venice, I forget. Probably my ignorance of Italian oenology. Or the fact that Valpolicella doesn't rhyme with Dante.

Even in 1954 Chianti was as well-known to the British as claret. A rustic wine, we were not amused by its presumption but greatly enjoyed its decorative qualities. Chelsea bedsits were lit by those straw-covered, podgy bottles converted into lamps. Fiascos they were called, and I remember one particular fiasco with special poignancy.

It was Carey's first visit to Tuscany. I and my family arrived at Florence in a hundred-degree heatwave – a big change from the three feet of snow experienced only a year before. Carey, then a rebellious thirteen-year-old, stood up Michelangelo for the Hotel Belvedere swimming pool. It was far too hot to argue, so my wife Sheila and I set out for the Bargello alone. We saw the Michelangelos. Then we fought for a table at Camillo, that year's trendy trattoria. Then we drank a two-litre fiasco of Chianti Classico. Next day, just as we were about to cool sore feet and sorer heads in the Belvedere pool, Carey announced that she was now ready for the Michelangelos.

SPANDA, RADDA IN CHIANTI

VITALI WEAVING, RADDA IN CHIANTI

It just goes to show that enjoyment of Tuscany should not be regimented; Thomas Cook pioneered his tours here, and he has a lot to answer for. Museums should be approached lightly, and discoveries made personally – with the intuitive pleasure which comes when one is truly touched by what one perceives. And how good it is to get out of the museums into fields, gardens, country churches, village piazzas, narrow streets, and vineyards. These vineyards – good year, bad year, come shine or come hail – seem to symbolize Tuscany's continuity, its fitness for survival.

From the converted tower in Radda where Carey and I

are staying, we look out upon this land not much different from the time of the Chianti League, winegrowers who installed themselves there in 1415. In the foreground spring leaves burgeon on the winestocks; middle distance, a pond with the vineyard reflected at sunset; background, a gentle slope reaches up towards the village on its inevitable hill. A Tuscan perspective not far removed from the burnt umber landscape in the background of Uccello's *Battle of San Romano*.

Our hosts at the tower, Lele and Augusto Vitali, have left a bottle of home-made wine to welcome us. She is large and maternal, he small and ascetic. Both as warm as the wine, and full of invitations to go over to their farmhouse for more of their own *vino rosso*. 'Everyone makes their own here – even, like us, with other people's grapes,' says Lele, in her excellent English, learned as a child from Irish nuns. Surprising they find the time: Augusto is an airforce officer serving at the War College in Florence, and Lele a weaver. From the loom in her home, she turns out sweaters and scarves to order – and there's always a glass of rough, strong wine for her clients.

Lele Vitali's brother, Giorgio Bianchi, has been Communist Mayor of Radda for eleven years. He is popular because seen to be a working winemaker, not an absentee landlord. 'Every Saturday my wife and I go to Rome and sell direct from a van,' says Giorgio. 'I work four hours a

RADDA IN CHIANTI

SANTA CRISTINA

day on the land – and the rest of the day, I'm mayor.'

Mayor Bianchi expresses new hope for Tuscany's unstable wine business, and agriculture in general. 'Outsiders are re-investing profits from industry. English, German, American and Italians from Milan. Milanese are foreigners here, too. I should know, I'm Milanese! The old Tuscan aristocracy have lost the battle.' But the Communist Mayor of Radda is no bigot; he gives praise where it's due, adding: 'With the notable exception of the Antinoris and the Frescobaldis.'

These noble winemakers have been in the game some 600 years; and they too will be appearing in the book. But let me make it clear: this is not a wine guide of Tuscany. It is a book of personal impressions of people and places. The wine of Tuscany seems a natural link between culture and countryside, between one age and another, between city-dweller and countryman. It is always there.

With *cittadini* and *contadini*, moving back and forth between town and country, Tuscany is constantly in motion. Town and country seem to merge in the landscape: as one approaches Siena, its three hills rise suddenly above a rolling wave of land like a ship in full sail; one can walk not too strenuously into delicious countryside from the very heart of Florence.

It is a landscape bathed in silence or vibrant with noise; Milanese writer Giorgio Soavi describes it as having the divine and innocent simplicity expressed in the poetry of Dante and the music of Monteverdi. In other words, art in natural surroundings – opera by a moonlit lake, a statue with pigeons perched on its head.

And in the wine's yearly cycle a reminder of Tuscany's continuity. Just when all seems lost and wintry, a natural renaissance takes place. And Tuscans over the years have responded to its call.

Julian More
Radda in Chianti 1986

LE CRETE

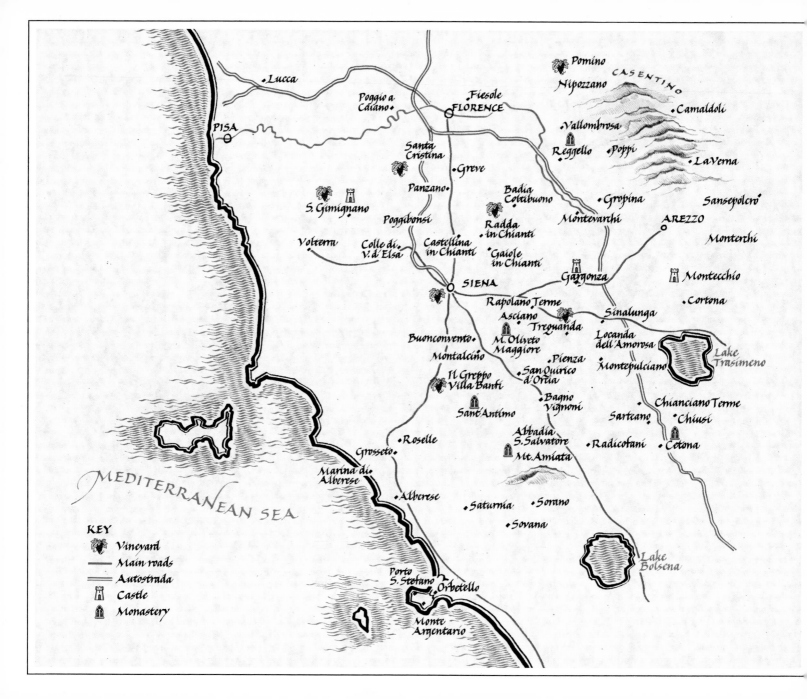

— PART I —
PLANTING

TUSCAN ROOTS

FLORENCE

On such a slope as this the Etruscans planted the first vine, brought with them from Asia Minor. Or so I like to think. Close to their ship in the creek below, on a south-facing slope, what more romantic spot for the origins of Enotria, the land of wine? Monte Argentario with a cool sea breeze, a few fleecy clouds – and complete stillness.

It is late spring. The film star villas shuttered up, beach colonies tactfully camouflaged by virginia creeper. And we have the narrow, unmetalled corniche road to ourselves.

From the roadside border of genista, cornflowers and poppies, the slope falls away through sturdy olive groves, meadows with fruit trees and clusters of cypresses. There is not much surface to the road, the hairpin bends are savage, and it's a nasty roll down to the little *calas*

MONTE ARGENTARIO

ROSELLE

From the Etruscan arrival in Italy to the first Medici, twenty-two centuries; from the Medicis to us, a mere five. Yet the Etruscans were the founders of Tuscan inventiveness. Engineers, sailors, traders, musicians, they were an exuberant, life-enhancing people whose decimation by the Romans I abhor as much as Lawrence.

Their sites cast an indefinable spell. At the ruins of Roselle I sense this familiar lightness, a happy déjà vu. Once an island, the Etruscan city of Roselle was built high on its hill for defence; now the Maremma coastal plain below is a hazy, golden sea of wheat. Nothing moves, not a bird, not a blade of grass; there is an uncanny stillness, not threatening as before a storm but with a warm resonance, while we explore the remains of a craftsman's cottage, circa 600 years before Christ.

indenting the promontory's rocky coastline. But the sea in those creeks has a blue-green clarity, seductive as a siren, like a dream of the Mediterranean long ago. A Homeric view.

'For in Homeric days a restlessness seems to have possessed the Mediterranean basin, and ancient races began shaking ships like seeds over the sea.' (D. H. Lawrence: *Etruscan Places*)

So little is known of the Etruscans, what does remain is tantalizing. The Romans wiped out all but their necropoli. They could not, however, destroy the fields nurtured by spilled Etruscan blood. Along the wild ridge road to Volterra, the view is forever to misty, indigo hills. And the light intensifies as we near Volterra, perched on its windy,

SANT' ANTIMO

perilous bluff overlooking the Maremma. Signs say CHAINS IN SNOW, but in May on either side of the road long, silky grass, rippled by the wind, stretches into the distance. These Elysian fields yield Etruscan artefacts as well as crops. Farmers around Volterra, ploughing, have regularly turned up pottery, gold leaf jewellery, rings and glass.

And tumuli yielded astonishing funeral urns. The decorative friezes and figures of these mysterious people reveal the humanity of their beliefs. Carved reliefs in alabaster, mined from the quarries near Volterra, show the afterlife as something to be looked forward to, a natural place to go, with palm trees and dolphins and loved ones. The puritan, logical Romans could not tolerate the Etruscan need for symbols, their free-spirited attitude to sex and death and religion.

Etruscan gods were there to guide, not judge. And the journey downward to death was not fearful. Just as the serpent god below the earth sent you surging into life, so the fish god below the waves brought you surging back

VOLTERRA

again. One god, the great navigator, with eyes in his wings and a double fish-tail, beautifully expresses this feeling of power without aggression.

Representations of the deceased are very down-to-earth. Foreshortened as two sphinxes, a husband and wife lie on top of a sarcophagus they presumably share. They're chatting together, she a bit bad-tempered. Did they go out with a final domestic tiff? There is an honesty about these Etruscan heads; lacking all classical nobility, they are more humane than the pompous busts of Roman senators and popes.

A Tuscan schoolboy, one of a group who suddenly take over Volterra's museum, filling it with shrill pandemonium, runs his hands over the stone with a kind of awe and wonder. Deep in the tactile experience, he seems to be in other-worldly communication with his ancestors.

If I could choose between descent from the Romans or Etruscans, I would choose the Etruscans any day.

Not that the Romans didn't leave a few good things in their usually disastrous wake. Their theatre at Fiesole

CASOLE D'ELSA

BADIA FIESOLANA

provides the best seat in town for the mountains of the Mugello in the changing light show of a summer evening. They are the mountains of approach – for the wicked barons of medieval times, rollicking down from their lairs for a quick sack and pillage; and now for the new barbarians of the north, tunnelling through by railway and autostrada to inflict themselves on Florence, as they wander listlessly from sight to sight, heads buried in Fodor, thighs burned red, and longing for an ice cream.

According to legend, Florence takes its name from Fiorino, that mythic Roman hero who defeated the rebel Catiline of Fiesole. But legend apart, its origins were a Roman settlement for army veterans at a spot blooming with flowers (*fiorente*-Firenze) by the Arno river. And Roman descent became a status symbol for early Florentines.

Where you came from and whose side you took caused many a vendetta and faction and war during the Tuscan Middle Ages. They read like play-offs for a sports event: Buondelmonti v. Amadei, Prato v. Pisa, Guelf v. Ghibelline, Donati v. Cerchi, Black v. White. The Blacks were descended from noble soldiers of the Roman army; the Whites were commoners, seed of the Etruscans. The chequerboard effect on church façades, such as the Badia Fiesolana, chronicles this division.

But my own particular pleasure in this period has nothing to do with violence. All over Tuscany are small Romanesque churches which have to be hunted for like white truffles. They are exquisite.

Early one morning, when the mists of the Arno swirl through twisty vineyards, we come upon the church of Gropina. Pigeons coo in the belltower, a cock crows and no one stirs behind the hamlet's grille windows. A gentle dog gives a few perfunctory woofs. The muddy farmyard has a Breughel look. Is it possible that so many wars could have passed this way?

ORBETELLO

GARGONZA

RIVER ARNO

Again at the Benedictine abbey of Sant' Antimo, the same sense of peace. A golden church in a green valley. And a cuckoo and nightingale singing together. It is time for the wall-eyed guardian's lunch. But willingly he lets us into the honey-gold, translucent interior, hastily delivering his tourist monologue in fractured German: '*Ecco la casa der Bischof! Wunderbar!*' A twelfth-century bishop actually lived upstairs. His apartment's walls have a repeated motif of hares gambolling in flowers, like hand-painted wallpaper. Downstairs, in the tiny crypt, we discover a touching fresco; in the light of our torch, an unknown artist's cherub, just face and wings, floats towards us from the darkness.

We give the guardian a lift up to the village of Castelnuovo dell' Abate, and buy a picnic – salami, broad beans, *pecorino* cheese, and fruit. The woman in the village shop has trouble slicing the salami and sighs '*Porca miseria!*' The world, she says, just has too many problems.

Ours is a tough one, too: where to have our picnic. In a meadow overlooking the church? Or further on, amid snapdragons, cistus, dog roses, alpine phlox, red clover, wild garlic? Or near volcanic craters forming a switchback green prairie as far as the eye can see? We settle for the shade of a great oak tree. A cock and hen pheasant, making love in the long grass nearby, spot us and depart with an indignant batting of wings.

Nature flourishes near these Romanesque churches. San Giusto in Salcio has farm buildings round the monastery. All Creatures Great And Small are here: pigs, lambs, one old priest and his two labourers. Our friend Lele gives us the facts of life about 'promiscuous husbandry', that ancient Tuscan farming method once carried out by the monks: 'Fruit trees are married to the vines. The vine is feminine (*La Vite*), the fruit trees are masculine (*Il Pero, Il Ciliegio*). One fruit tree can support several vines.' Occasionally a little vineyard-cum-orchard, untouched by mechanization, still has this medieval look.

SAN GIUSTO

PORTO S. STEFANO

SIENA

But the medieval look to end all is the city of Siena. Untouched by mechanization? Hardly. Even as I read that welcoming Latin inscription over a gate, 'Siena opens wide its heart to you', a juggernaut bus hurtles towards me; there's not room in the narrow street for both of us, so I dart sharply into a *barberia* for a shave I don't need. A close one.

A cloudburst has cleared the Campo of sodden souvenir-sellers, children chase pigeons from the puddles, and in the narrow streets behind the Duomo shafts of sunlight hit the washed, shiny surface. An old man with a straw-covered demijohn emerges to get a fill-up of Chianti Colli Senesi.

Soft Siena, stony Florence? That's what they say. But Siena always seems flinty enough to me. Take the riders in the Palio: a local *ragazzo*, jeans swapped for medieval costume, stamps out a cigarette on the cobblestones, mounts his bare-back steed, and dices with death in the gruelling race.

The two great cities have always been fierce rivals. But Siena succeeded first, thanks to its special relationship with the Holy Roman Emperors, and reached its financial and commercial zenith in the twelfth century. Its look is boom town Gothic: the miraculous façade of the Duomo by Pisano; a full moon rising behind the crenellations of the Palazzo Pubblico; a candlelit procession with the bells

SIENA

SIENA

As I look at Cimabue's *Crucifixion*, much of it irreparably damaged by the 1966 flood, it strikes me how tenuous the thread of Tuscany's survival has always been. Natural hazards were as frequent as man-made. In 1304 the Arno broke its banks, bringing down the Carraia Bridge, while people were watching a pageant depicting Hell. As the poet-philosopher Dante made nearly half his Inferno's inhabitants godless Florentines, he must have seen this mass drowning as the wrath of God made flesh – a revenge for obsession with the Mighty Florin, that gold coin with the lily of Florence stamped on the back.

> The evil flower
> Which leads the lambs and the sheep astray
> Because it has made a wolf of the shepherd

In 1348 God struck again – this time with the Black Death. Boccaccio pioneered medical description by his first-hand, gruelling account: '. . . in men and women alike it first betrayed itself by the emergence of certain tumours in the groin and the armpits, some of which grew as large as a common apple, others as an egg . . .'

To escape the Plague, Boccaccio's young bloods and their girlfriends meet in Santa Maria Novella and take to the hills of Fiesole where they divert themselves, 'embowered in shrubberies of various hues', by telling each other tales for ten days. Hence the title *The Decameron*.

of Siena ringing when Duccio's *Maestà*, most human of Sienese paintings, was first carried through the streets to the cathedral.

Duccio's Florentine contemporary, Cimabue, was also an innovator. Religious art began to reflect the greater flexibility of the Church: in the great Byzantine works of the so-called Dark Ages, the Virgin Mary had been a Queen; now she was La Mamma. Cimabue followed the call of God in nature, as St Francis of Assisi had done – and his figures have real flesh tints.

SIENA

Some are told with typical Tuscan bawdiness. Lecherous clerics and sex-mad nuns are often the butt of the humour. An abbott in trying to seduce a peasant's wife reassures her: '. . . hereby is my holiness no wise diminished, for holiness resides in the soul, and this which I ask you is but a sin of the flesh.'

Boccaccio made fun of the Church; Dante was the scourge of the commercial class. By 1338 with a population of 90,000 – bigger than London – Florence was Europe's richest city. From a counter in a narrow street – *il banco* – the moneylenders operated, and this was the

POMINO

beginning of modern banking. Florentine power began to be felt abroad. 'As bankers we opened a London office in 1234,' Leonardo Frescobaldi tells me, as though it were last week. 'We lent so much money to your King, he gave us concessions for Cornish tin and Scottish wool. The English nobles were furious and chased us out. In revenge we took over distribution of Bordeaux wine, and cut off supplies to England. Think of them! Without claret, poor things! Then your King Edward III didn't pay back his debts and we went bankrupt. We were obliged to develop the land we'd bought with our bank profits – and became winemakers.'

What the Frescobaldis did, naturally the Antinoris did at much the same time. In 1385 the first Antinori was enrolled in the Vintner's Guild of Florence.

Tradition adapts easily, however. Today's enterprising head of the firm, Piero Antinori, introduces me to Tignanello, a revolutionary red wine made on their Santa Cristina estate. 'That's Chianti Classico country,' he tells me, over an informal lunch in the Cantinetta Antinori, a cool, stylish restaurant in their Florence *palazzo*. 'But Tignanello is not made with the traditional blend of four grapes. Only Sangiovese are used, plus twenty per cent Cabernet – a complete innovation in Tuscan wines. I only make the wine in good years, so it can age. Another new wine, Solaia, is made with just Cabernet.'

SIENA

SORANO

BROLIO

PLANTING

GARZONA

Previously, in towns like San Gimignano which once had seventy towers (now only thirteen), they would outdo each other in skyscraping; towers were later limited by law to ninety-six feet. A blow to baronial egos which they never survived.

The first days of his exile Dante spent in the tower of Gargonza, a fairytale thirteenth-century castle deep in a wooded game reserve, where our car nearly collided with two giant porcupines. The unfortunate Dante idealized love in the divine form of Beatrice and his country in the unrealistic form of cultural unification. A humanist ahead of his time, he abhorred war and believed in the values of Greek democracy, a true liaison of the classes. Not the bourgeois democracy of Florence, in which being on the wrong side of a corridor of power meant instant banishment. Such was Dante's fate. Luckily for us, it inspired *The Divine Comedy*.

Such eclecticism in winemaking seems to deny the Tuscan reputation for *campanilismo*, only seeing as far as the view from your own belltower.

Medieval narrow-mindedness was beginning to die out, even in the days when the Antinoris and Frescobaldis began making wine. The new bourgeoisie kept the old feudal ogres in order by insisting they lived in Florence, where their rollicking and violence could be controlled.

A descendant of another Florentine writer, the historian Guicciardini, is the present owner of Gargonza. Gangly, bespectacled Roberto Guicciardini spends the weekend here, the week in Florence where he has a mass of projects. And where his wife Teresa works in her

SAN GIMIGNANO

family's musical instrument shop. Together they have lovingly restored the castle's main buildings into a cultural centre, and converted numerous *foresterie* into self-catering apartments. These two-bathroom peasant cottages attract simple-lifers from New York, London, Munich and Rome. 'We have a Buddhist TV writer who has been here all winter,' Roberto tells me. 'Must be vegetarian. He never goes near our restaurant.'

'Won't you come and starve with us?' is Teresa's charmingly eccentric invitation to dinner in the kitchen. The Florentines have a reputation for stinginess, but dinner in the Guicciardini kitchen turns out to be no starving matter. Teresa knocks up a spicy concoction of tomatoes, eggs and rice; and Roberto opens a bottle of 1974 Chianti Classico in our honour. He's afraid it may be too old, but it is still velvety smooth. We eat off a table fixed up by one of Teresa's musical instrument repairers. 'Florentine craftsmen like taking on a job in a different field. It's a challenge.' Budgerigars fly loose in the room; one has got out, but Roberto is sure it will home.

Carey and I are still in the thirteenth century, as we awake next morning at Gargonza with rooks cawing in the chestnut trees, a woody smell wafting through cell-like windows, and a smoky sunrise over the Valdichiana.

On the other side of the valley, just south of Arezzo, is quite a different castle. You enter by secret code – a number of buzzes on the entryphone. 'Otherwise I would get tourists all the time,' explains the sole occupant of Montecchio, Olietta Budini-Gattai, a lively young woman from Rome with eager, piercing brown eyes. Her few grey hairs mark the battles she has had with the authorities while restoring the eighth-century tower, gargantuan boundary walls, and her own modest house with bath in the bedroom to avoid knocking down a main wall. Olietta has won awards for her restoration.

'I don't like the word castle,' she says. '*Terra Murata* – land with walls – sounds less warlike. There used to be fifty houses like mine, all the way round the interior walls. And two churches. Eventually I want it to have that community feeling again. The Keep will be a workshop for artists. The town planners hate me for living in a fortress, so I must prove to them I'm not some despot by opening to the public. But I have years of work yet.'

The fourteenth-century owner, English *condottiere* Sir John Hawkwood, had no such hassles with the Arezzo town planners. Hired by Florence to capture Arezzo in 1384, he was rewarded with the gift of Montecchio.

Sir John was also posthumously awarded a fresco in the Florence Duomo by that avant-garde master Uccello, who still looks modern today. Astonishing that with so few years of peace – a mere ten in Tuscany's Middle Ages – creativity should have flourished as it did.

MONTECCHIO

DUOMO, FLORENCE

Humanity, teamwork, and science were its hallmarks.

Brunelleschi ran into labour problems, when building the cathedral's dome. He hired and fired with Florentine toughness; but also, with Florentine practicality, provided a canteen for the workers – in the dome! With wine, too. You needed a good head for heights.

Just across from Florence rail station is Santa Maria Novella, which, while tourist buses are hurtling round the Duomo in both directions, is a cultural haven of peace. Marginally fewer sweaty bodies compete for viewing space around Giotto's *Crucifix*. And it is possible to contemplate for a few moments the humanity of Masaccio's master-work *Holy Trinity*, completed just one year before his death aged twenty-seven. In that short life, Masaccio's realism brought religious art out of the clouds.

Moving on to the Carmine, we find the Brancacci Chapel wrapped in plastic for restoration of newly dis-covered Masaccio frescoes; it looks just as if the modern sculptor Christo had 'packaged' it. And suddenly Masaccio seems all the more relevant to our days: he shows eyes with pain in them, unpretty bodies, a deep compassion for human fragility. These were already modern times.

In 1434, a mere two years before Uccello's tribute to Sir John Hawkwood, Cosimo de' Medici, leader of the busi-ness community, became uncrowned king of Florence. And the Renaissance reached its vintage years.

S. Maria Novello, Florence

ASCIANO

S. QUIRICO D'ORCIA

San Guisto alle Monache

— PART II —
FLOWERING

THE GOLDEN AGE OF THE MEDICIS

FLORENCE

We Western Europeans chauvinistically tend to forget that not everyone was going through Dark Ages when we were. Constantinople was a thriving cultural centre; it was Byzantine scholars who brought humanism to Italy. And Byzantine influence – oriental in architecture, iconographic in painting – paved the way for experimentation and a different beauty in art.

The Italian Renaissance was a new approach to the best in ancient Greek and Roman culture, which had been kept alive in the Byzantine Empire. Art historians claim it for art, humanists for thought, and economists for capitalism. In fact, in Florence it was a combination of all three; one of those happy historical coincidences when creative talent and a search for knowledge had the money to support them in the style to which they are seldom accustomed.

SOVANA

VALLOMBROSA

This wealthy banker and textile merchant found favour by a reputation for benevolence. He guided the city's government rather than ruled it. And with regal status achieved by the grandness of his life style, he became a sort of throne behind the power.

With the Medicis a classroom label was born: Benevolent Despot.

There's a mood about that label, at least. As we drive down to Valdarno from Vallombrosa, a vast, crumbling mansion catches my eye near Reggello. We stop. Another eerie silence of the Tuscan outback, broken suddenly by an approaching phut-phut. A man on a Vespa stops to tell us this was a Medici farm. I feel a strange excitement that those very gnarled and twisted old olive trees might have been planted in Medici times.

With Florence's fifteenth-century wealth and know-how, the natural scepticism of commerce replaced the accepted dogmas of the Church. Also there was an intense civic pride. It was sweet to do a deal for one's city state; the mercenaries like Sir John Hawkwood could do the dying.

Thus the natural leaders came not from Church, nobility, or military; but from the merchant class. And who could have been more natural than Cosimo de' Medici?

Cosimo the businessman ran his Bruges and Avignon branches by an imaginative system of incentive: his managers had no salary but a high percentage of profits. Before the advent of Telex, he kept in regular contact with them by daily messenger service, an astonishing team of riders and runners shuttling between Florence and Avignon with the memoes.

REGELLO

FLORENCE

FLORENCE

PONTE VESPUCCI, FLORENCE

Cosimo's own profits were ploughed back into town and country property.

The great grey-brown stone blocks of Renaissance *palazzi* can be overwhelming in the narrow streets and poky piazzas of Florence. Such solid, grandiose architecture needs space to do it justice.

Five minutes up the Via Bolognese from the Piazza della Libertà, I turn off the noisy, narrow street, past a gatekeeper in a raffish hat, his grin tipsy with mischief. Suddenly I am in the country. A long driveway stretches to the fifteenth-century Villa La Pietra, cypress-lined in perfect perspective as far as the goldeny ochre façade. On either side, there are hay and roses beneath the cypresses; rows of vines alternate with olives and fruit trees. 'The olives are profitable,' says the villa's owner, Sir Harold Acton, greeting us in a huge, dark drawing room with art treasures looming from the shadows. 'Sometimes the smell of pig is a little tiresome.'

Neighbours: a pig-owning convent on one side, Sorbonne students at the Villa Finaly on the other. Each summer the French students perform a Goldoni play in the famous Acton garden, restored by Sir Harold's father from English herbaceous borders ('They never work in this climate') to its original, based on designs by the son of Renaissance artist, Giorgio Vasari. An eighteenth-century feature was added: statuary imported from tumbledown Veneto villas – charming figures of valets, maids with flowers, a piccolo player, a hunter punishing his dog. A perfect setting for Goldoni.

Sir Harold leads us down shady avenues quite spryly for his eighty-two years, despite the heat and a good thick suit with waistcoat and Windsor-knotted tie. American on his mother's side, writer, collector, scholar, courteous host, keen gardener, he seems perfectly at ease, alone in his vast Renaissance home. But it does have problems, which are perhaps not like yours or mine. 'One of the five gardeners set fire to the place the other day,' he confides. 'And I had

FONTARRONCO

a footman who stole from me, so he had to go too. One's terrified of burglary, you know. So many of these old houses are on the market. Nobody wants them, nobody can afford the upkeep. Alice Keppel and Mercedes Huntington, English and Americans were my father's neighbours. All gone . . .'

I catch a sudden, astonishing glimpse of the cathedral dome through the box hedges. Is that Florence? So near? For a moment it had felt very, very far away. A sweet melancholy hangs over La Pietra. Like the last Medici, the last Acton has no heir to inherit it, and he has been a friendly figure on its landscape for many years. In 1986 he was made an honorary citizen of Florence. 'About time,' he says quietly. 'I've lived here since I was born.'

Renaissance country estates have their problems, too. Statues green with moss, fountains clogged and silent. But occasionally comes a Venetian industrialist like Zonin to make a profitable wine business out of an estate like Pian d'Albola in the rolling Chianti hills.

However grand the house – and Pian d'Albola is *la vie de château* – the vineyard comes right up to its terraces. It is a working farm, not just a show place, so the *casa padronale*, the boss's house, is separated from its vineyard by a rough road on which a tractor stands.

The front façade has a rounded belltower atop the centre of the roof. In front of the chapel, a huge wine barrel converted into a dog kennel, and solar-heated swimming pool (twentieth century). Horses in a tree-lined paddock will carry *il padrone* and guests to the boar hunt, through gates crowned with figures of Bacchus and Athene.

What a let down is the unlived-in, tourist monument in comparison! The state of the Medici villa Poggio a Caiano is a regional disgrace. There's all the difference between the warm twilight glow of melancholy dilapidation, and a shambolic garden and grotto smelling of urine. Based on a traditional Roman villa design adapted by Giuliano da Sangallo, it is the only extant building whose construction

SAN GUISTO ALLE MONACHE

FLORENCE FROM SAN DOMENICO

was personally directed by Lorenzo de' Medici, Cosimo's grandson. He is, no doubt, turning in his grave.

Real estate took a large proportion of Medici profits. So did art patronage. Apart from a taste for collection, the Medicis suffered from usurer's guilt, rich man's remorse, a bad night after a good day at the bank. Banking was the sin of usury. In matters of charity, the Medicis paid more than lip service to the Church. And further atoned by financing beautiful objects for all people to enjoy.

The Church had been the patron of religious art, now the Medicis were patrons of civic art. Statues told symbolic tales of Florence's military triumphs over French kings or popes or Milanese dukes: David, the slayer of Goliath, is treated differently by Michelangelo, Donatello and Verrocchio. To the formality of Greek classicism is added a Tuscan suppleness and vitality. Donatello's David looks like a cocky country boy who has just killed a wild boar with a catapult.

The young Michelangelo, brought up among stonemasons and said to have been weaned on milk with granite in it, worked on a faun in one of Lorenzo's gardens. Lorenzo thought the teeth too good for an old faun, so Michelangelo broke them down a bit. He would not be so obliging later on.

Under the patronage of the Medicis the artisan became courtier – with star temperament to match. The deeply spiritual Michelangelo quarrelled endlessly with the materialistic Pope Julius. Stony Florence, with its hard heads and spiritual complexities, God in uneasy alliance with Mammon. The quarries of Carrara had never been busier, the hand of Lorenzo the Magnificent was forever digging deeper into his purse.

Lorenzo was that rarity, a merchant prince with artistic talent. As a poet he evoked country matters in the bawdiest of rhymes, and won favour with the *populo minuto* by appearing to be one of the boys. His obscene carnival songs occasionally gave way to simple, prophetic verse:

> How passing fair is youth
> For ever fleeting away;
> Who happy would be, let him be;
> Of tomorrow who can say?

In the golden age of its culture, Florence was paradoxically past its economic prime. Lorenzo's power needed a healthy cash flow to be wielded effectively; it was all very well to have Botticelli's *Prima Vera* on his wall and a crowd of bitchy humanists under his roof and bills for books which took half the State's revenue. Culture alone is notoriously powerless. Hell-fire preacher Savonarola harangued the people into an anti-Medici fervour, and after Lorenzo's death the Medicis were exiled in 1494.

PIAZZA DE S. TRINITA, FLORENCE

PHARMACY, CAMALDOLI

But in spite of deaths and exiles and assassinations the Medicis long outlived Savonarola's Republic. By shifty diplomacy, they managed to get a pope or two in the family. Very handy in a crisis. After the Florentine conquest of Siena in 1559, the Pope made another Cosimo de' Medici Grand Duke of Tuscany. And the three great cities – Florence, Arezzo and Siena – were unified for the first time.

Artists of all kinds continued to rise in the world with the Medicis. A little of their patrons' toughness in negotiating rubbed off on them: Donatello refused a Medici farm in lieu of payment, because farmers' incessant moans about weather and taxes bored him. Not all were as pious as their paintings, either: Carmelite monk Fra Filippo Lippi, whose *Annunciation* portrays such serenity in its vine-arboured cloister, seduced a model posing for the Virgin Mary, and had a son by her.

A favourite of mine is the sculpture of the della Robbia family, who put vitreous glazing on to terra cotta. Its pursuit can lead to disappointment: in Santa Croce Andrea's lovely boy carrying a fish is difficult to see; in the Bargello, his genius Uncle Luca's *Madonna* could do with a good dust. But at La Verna, Andrea's *Annunciation* and *Adoration of the Child* are seen to perfection.

The journey to La Verna is in itself a pilgrimage. Driving up into the mountains of the Casentino, we reach Camaldoli, a cool retreat for summer-fried Florentines. At the sixteenth-century pharmacy – old bottles and china jars, exotic herbal smells – Carey buys a herb tea for her liver. She finds she doesn't need it, for now the road becomes a real shaker, twisting up little valleys, up over ridges where miles and miles away high clouds cast dark patches on the sunlit pine forests. Now we are in the darkness of such a forest, bumping along a track that doesn't seem to lead anywhere, then suddenly opens up to a metalled road again, then more dirt track, and finally we reach La Verna.

MONTEVARCHI

MONTE OLIVETO MAGGIORE

S. Quirico d'Orcia

A few more liver-shaking bumps along the cobbled road to the Franciscan monastery, and we park in the shade of a deep, dark birch-and-fir forest. We are the only visitors. A Sister selling postcards directs us to a Brother who shows us where the Church is. There are no signs – except SILENZIO. In the church, my heels on marble sound like a Spanish dancer's, and I approach the della Robbias on tip-toe to avoid disrupting a Brother's devotions. It has been worth every bump of the journey.

Not all monasteries have this pleasurable ambiance. In the over-restored, red-brick abbey of Monte Oliveto Mag-giore – garden suburb Renaissance – a monk in housework habit passes with a packet of Omo, a sign reads YOU ARE NOT ALLOWED TO BEHAVE INDECENTLY. Long before it was an antiseptic tourist attraction, American art historian Bernard Berenson came here, braving the chilly winter of these windswept craters, to seek out the frescoes of Sig-norelli and Sodoma.

Berenson wrote of how to look at paintings: 'One moment is enough, if the concentration is absolute. We must look and look till we live in the painting and for a moment become identified with it. If we do not succeed in loving what through the ages has been loved, it is useless to lie ourselves into believing that we do. A good rough test is whether we feel it is reconciling us with life.' (*The Italian Painters Of The Renaissance*)

In front of Piero della Francesca's *Risen Christ at Sansepolcro*, for instance. Kenneth Clark describes Him as 'This country god . . .', reconciling us not only with life but the very pagan roots of the Tuscan people.

At the tiny chapel of Monterchi, here too I sense the truth of Berenson's test, a spiritual link between subject and surroundings in Piero's *Madonna del Parto*. The Virgin Mary is a proud, pregnant girl who could be from the village across the road; she's showing off her big belly to two angels with determined, peasant faces. Just like three girls on a Saturday *passeggiata* in Arezzo.

MADONNA DEL PARTO, MONTERCHI

CEMETERY, MONTERCHI

PIAZZA DELLA SIGNORIA

Outside, an old lady from the village grabs my arm: '*Molto bella? No?*' Eager for my assurance that I had liked the fresco, she then tells me in agonized tones that there are plans for it to be sold to an American museum.

Perhaps it was just a rumour, I tell her. Perhaps it would be too hard to move. I cannot console her. Piero's fresco is as much part of her locality and life as the house she lives in.

I fail the Berenson test with most of the statuary in the Piazza della Signoria. It's altogether too monumental and forbidding. Gross bodies with dainty genitalia; that great white *Neptune* by Ammanati, gushing away over his sea horses. But, of course, there is the notable exception: Benvenuto Cellini's *Perseus*.

All the more poignant is this admirable statue, since reading of its making in Benvenuto's swashbuckling auto-biography, the best contemporary description of Medici patronage. Statue and book show the other side of the Florentine coin: its violence, quick to flare up, quick to subside.

This soldier-goldsmith drew his sword at the slightest insult, and was paranoid about potential enemies. ('They were planning to put some powdered diamond in my food.') But of Cosimo I's patronage he could be sure, and offered to make the Grand Duke his Perseus for board and lodging only. Perseus represents the Medicis; for all Florence to see, he triumphantly holds up the severed head of Medusa, who represents the defeated Republic.

The final casting of the statue has great suspense in the telling. Benvenuto's team of bronze-founders, carpenters,

AREZZO

FLORENCE

labourers, even housemaids work through the night, while Benvenuto in despair that there might not be enough metal, hurls his own pewter plates into the mould.

Castigator of pretentious second-rate artists, Benvenuto was lavish in praise of genius: 'The splendid Leonardo had chosen to show a battle scene, with horsemen fighting together and standards being captured, and he had drawn it magnificently.'

Leonardo da Vinci saw the Renaissance not as a rebirth but a new birth. Greek and Latin were unimportant in the dissecting of human bodies: what were people living *now* made of? He was impatient with the Medici obsession with classical values: 'The painter will produce pictures of little merit if he takes the works of others as his standard; but if he will apply himself to learn from the objects of nature, he will produce good results.'

A bird in flight, a premonition of the airplane. It was no alchemist's spell that made a bird fly, nor cosmic theory. Why it flew had to be proved by experiment. 'I wish to work miracles,' Leonardo said.

Little short of miracle-workers, Tuscans of the Renaissance discovered perspective, composed the first opera, pioneered political science, and at Pienza invented modern town planning. As I walk down the Via de L'Amore and back up the Via della Fortuna, it strikes me how advanced in every way were the days of the Medicis. Then I remember an astonishing date. 1564. The year Michelangelo died, Shakespeare was born.

Piazza della Signoria

RADDA IN CHIANTI

PART III

RIPENING

THE AGE OF UNREASON

SANMEZZANO

The ripening of a grape is a delicate operation. A freak hail storm can wipe out an entire vineyard's crop. Too much rain, mildew sets in. Too little, the grapes are puny. Then there's that nasty relation of the greenfly, *Phylloxera*, which can destroy a whole region's viticulture.

The great vintage years of Tuscany seemed to be over. Though in some areas of endeavour it continued to ripen healthily, its seventeenth and eighteenth centuries suffered a kind of midsummer madness. Over-ripening, it might be called. And in some cases downright rot.

I'm reminded of it one Sunday at the Flower Festival of Greve in the very heart of Chianti. Greve has a fine seventeenth-century feature – the Piazza Matteotti. Dispensing with Renaissance symmetry, its porticoed buildings have the informal, easy-going look of a prosperous

CASOLE D'ELSA

S. AMBROGIO MARKET, FLORENCE

market town. Beneath the arcades, a stunning spectrum of colour. Prize azaleas, pelargoniums, marguerites. But no hard-sell from the stall-holders. A most low-key *festa*, this. Carey roams here and there with her camera; no one takes much notice of her. What's up? Normally Tuscans love to have their picture taken: at a salami-and-cheese stall, a small boy does not have the usual grin of expectancy, nor his father a salesman's smile. At the vegetable stall, the old lady in black has no green beans, no lettuce, no baby marrow. 'Chernobyl,' she says – and the mystery is solved.

An ill wind has blown Russia's radiation over Italy.

Banner headlines in *La Nazione* cast a blight on the Flower Festival, and I wonder about the milk in my *cappuccino*. Something rotten in the state of Tuscany all those years ago seems trivial compared to our world-threatening ecological disasters. Yet this beautiful seventeenth-century market-place suddenly becomes a grim reminder: science has come a long way since Tuscany's greatest scientist, Galileo, discovered Jupiter's satellites in 1610.

They were known as the Medicean Planets, and Galileo became mathematician royal to Cosimo II. Ironical that just when they should have planets named after them, the Medicis' own star was beginning to fade. In fact Galileo was one of the few bright stars where only a century ago there had been a galaxy.

The rationalist Galileo was naturally at odds with the Church. And the Inquisition sniffed out heresy like police dogs in search of drugs. Not even a Medici could prevent the persecution of scientists, and Galileo's manuscripts had to be hidden in a haystack. His worst sin was agreement with the Copernican heresy that the earth moved round the sun. The Church still reckoned the earth to be the centre of God's universe, about which every other planet turned. So the Inquisition banned Galileo's work. Later, deciding his own research was too important to be prevented by heroics, he officially renounced his support

GREVE

for Copernicus. But after the Inquisitors had heard him, he is said to have muttered: 'It still keeps moving!'

The earth moved, while Florence went spinning into its own orbit of frivolity. The first fireworks appeared – wooden statues with mouths and eyes pouring flames and sparks. The Spectacular was born with shows employing actors, musicians, painters, scientists, and balletic horses. A painting showed nymphs castrating the Grand Duke's dwarf. The wild boys played *calcio*, the first form of football. And the Medicis played practical jokes with trick fountains that drenched their guests.

In art and architecture there was a yearning for sensationalism. As Harold Acton writes of baroque monuments in *The Last Medici*: 'A building, unless it administered a definite shock or, like an electric fish, a momentary concussion, was more or less doomed to failure.'

Baroque art was even more gaudy than Pontormo who, among other Mannerists, had paved the way for its excesses: 'The Madonna is wearing a two-toned pinky purple dress with peach-coloured sleeves . . . A simpering, rouged, idiot Child sits on the Madonna's lap.' (Mary McCarthy: *The Stones of Florence*). The essence of Catholic kitsch – like the modern Saint Rita I saw in Santo Spirito with electric light bulbs round her, a sickly nun who slopes sideways in ecstasy like a crooner on the cover of Thirties sheet-music.

MONTALCINO

SIENA

ALBERESE

ALBERESE

That crusty eighteenth-century Scottish doctor, Smollett, did not approve: 'Besides numberless pictures of flagellation, crucifixion and descent from the Cross, we have Judith with the head of Holofernes, Herodias with the head of John the Baptist, Jael assassinating Sisera in his sleep, Peter writhing on the Cross, Stephen battered with stones, Sebastian stuck full of arrows, Laurence frying on a gridiron, Batholomew flayed alive, and a hundred other pictures equally frightful.'

The last Medici of any importance, Cosimo III, was a religious fanatic. Harold Acton describes his own book on the subject as 'Very Florentine' – in other words, highly *caustico* about Cosimo. 'A devotee to the point of bigotry; intolerant of all free thought; hated by his wife; his existence a round of visits to churches and convents, a daily routine of prostration at different altars.'

Here was a moral vigilante, using the ethics of the Middle Ages to try to stop the rot. His French wife was caught tickling the cook; he accused her dancing master of bigamy. Making a cardinal of his playboy brother, Gian Carlo, for political reasons, Cosimo singularly failed to deprive the cardinal of his harem, which included a Christian Turkish slave called Ottomana.

Frustrated in his failure to put his own house in order, Cosimo had Jews flayed alive in winter for visiting Christian whores. Prostitutes had to have passports; they were flung into the notorious Stinche prison for the mildest misdemeanour. And he issued an edict against the 'improper amours' of Florentine youth.

Understandably unhappy in love himself, Cosimo compensated by a gargantuan appetite. Preaching abstinence in others, he bloated himself on snow-cooled food and drink. Then, over-ripening to excess, went on vigorous hunting expeditions and crash diets.

This duality of indulgence and frugality in one body is a good metaphor for Florence in its decadent, poverty-stricken days of the eighteenth century. There was one more powerless Medici to go. Poor Gian Gastone had a stab at reducing the tyranny of the Church and persecution of minorities, then gave up and took to his bed like Oblomov. With his death in 1737, Tuscany passed to the Austrian House of Lorraine.

The last Medici? Not quite. As I've ended Cosimo's tale on a gastronomic note, let me now write of Lorenza de' Medici, very much alive and cooking.

Former food editor of Italian *Vogue*, Donna Lorenza, descendant by a lateral branch, certainly lives and works in Medici style. Married to businessman Piero Stucchi-Prinetti, she is hostess of Badia a Coltibuono (Abbey of the Good Harvest), a vast property dating from the seventh century and producing wine for nearly a thousand years.

Beneath a magnolia tree in the abbey's neat, maze-like

S. QUIRICO D'ORCIA

garden of box hedges and arbours, I sip a Bianco di Coltibuono, straw-coloured with a tinge of green; it certainly lives up to its reputation of 'fresh floral aroma and well-balanced acidity'.

Donna Lorenza gives Tuscan country cooking courses in her own home. Chefs and cooking teachers come from as far as California: Tante Marie's Cooking School of San Francisco, The Perfect Pan School of Cooking in San Diego. Living like Donna Lorenza's houseguests, they go to neighbouring castles for gourmet dinners, which they certainly wouldn't do at just any old cookery school, and return home with a taste for Tuscan high life.

Tuscan cuisine has a shaky reputation with us foreigners, based largely on the horrors of demi-pension. Who wants to eat where they're staying – compulsorily? Happily it's now becoming a choice in the brighter hotels and *pensiones*. 'They cannot afford good chefs,' explains the owner of Celestino, a fine trattoria near the Ponte Vecchio with no such problems. We have fled there to escape one more ghastly dinner at an otherwise charming hotel in an olive grove, where our waiter snapped at a French guest who complained about the soggy Gnocchi: 'Let's stop this morbid conversation!'

My advice is stick to *cucina povera*, and you won't go hungry. It means 'cooking of the poor', but it's now popular in middle-class homes. Lele Vitali, her husband

Augusto, twin sons of twenty, another son of twenty-four, his girlfriend are like an orchestra to feed. And tonight the Vitalis are augmented by a Belgian art historian, his wife, Carey and me.

The main dish of the impromptu Vitali dinner is *panzanelle*, deep-fried dough with a sauce of carrots, onions, tomatoes and olive oil. It's a very friendly dish, served in the middle of the table for all to dip into. Then there's *fagioli alla toscana*, beans cooked with celery and onions, and *crostata*, a cake from San Gimignano. 'We all have our own recipes,' says Lele. 'In winter, I'd give

MONTALCINO

BADIA A COLTIBUONO

CENTRAL MARKET, FLORENCE

you *ribollita* to warm you up – black cabbage and bread soup.'

Panzanelle, by the way, should not be confused with *panzanella*, that delicious salad of bread soaked in water and olive oil, with basil, tomatoes and onions.

Often the cheaper restaurants are the best. At the Ristorante Carloni, Gaiole: *tagliatelle*, *bistecca alla fiorentina*, chocolate mousse, unlimited local wine – at less than half the London cost. Not exactly cooking of the poor, either. Same thing at the Ristorante Pitena, near Montevarchi, where a notice reads FORBIDDEN TO SMOKE STRONG AND PERFUMED TOBACCO. Two huge family parties are noisily celebrating First Communions, with much hilarious speech-making and popping of Asti Spumante corks.

And to complete the evening, our waiter runs after Carey with her tip. 'Not enough?' she asks, used to Paris. 'Too much.' Italians do not respect overtipping, and in a country restaurant like this, service is included in the *coperto*; Carey should just have rounded up to the nearest convenient figure. 'I did not do anything special!' says the waiter.

Tuscan food sometimes gets the better of culture. All round the city, Lucca has red-brick ramparts, tree-lined for a shady walk and wide enough for a football game. It has gracious living in eighteenth-century hillside villas with English parks (terrible sign-posting – hunger forced us to give up the search), and the cosy elegance of an English cathedral town. But it also has something totally Tuscan: *valdestana*. What better lunch than this snack of light flaky pastry with tomato and salami? And for afters, *tutti-frutti* from the Gelateria Veneta, an ice cream-lover's paradise, which displays silver cups for Quality, Colour, and Courtesy.

I award my own cup for courtesy to restaurateur Carlo Citterio who puts up with our working clothes as though they were the height of Florentine fashion. Carlo, owner

FLORENCE

CENTRAL MARKET, FLORENCE

CENTRAL MARKET, FLORENCE

LOCANDA DELL' AMOROSA

a co-operative wine with three other winegrowers, each providing a different variety of grape.

But tonight Carlo is working as lighting designer; he hares about killing a floodlight here, switching one on there, to get just the right effect for Carey's night-shoot in the courtyard. The seventeenth-century chapel is lit up inside, the door left open. A German guest is politely removed from the court-yard, together with the giant white parasols, to show off a red-brick loggia in its pristine Renaissance state.

'The nice thing about being a photographer,' says Carey after the shoot, 'is people expect you to look a mess.' With impeccable manners, Carlo says he won't bother to shave for dinner or put on a clean shirt. Even though his other dinner guests are a modish *signora* who manages a health spa at Chianciano Terme and her smart Roman friend.

of the Locanda dell'Amorosa at Sinalunga, has turned his family country house into a top-class restaurant. 'I don't want to be in *Relais et Châteaux*,' he laughs. 'Who needs people threatening to take your star away? This is not a hotel anyway, it's a country house – with a few simple rooms, so my guests don't have to drive home. They can drink as much as they like.' The wine is naturally his own – a light, fruity *vino da tavola*. He is also experimenting:

Carlo's menu is original, offering such rarities as Wild Boar Sausage, Dandelion Salad, and Slices of Duck in Olive Sauce. It looks as if *cucina povera* is becoming chic. A dish translated as 'Fresh Water in Tomato Sauce' sounds just a little too poor till Carlo explains: 'The printer left out the "Fish".' But he does have genuine *zuppa ribollita*, and the spa lady and her Roman friend gush like Saturnia's hot springs about the merits of eating 'poor'.

Locanda dell' Amorosa

FLORENCE

Now the rich are eating 'poor', what are the poor eating? The grey, pinched faces of some of the elderly war-survivors in Florence's *zona popolare* have a look of permanent deprivation, as though hunger has become a habit. Not so the Santa Cristina vineyard workers, who are brown as nuts and sturdy as oak trees.

As it is mid-May the vines have budded and the Antinori workers are training them along the wires, three strands one above the other. From very old peasant families, they have faces of figures in the paintings: high cheekbones, keen eyes, sensuous mouths. Their humour is caustic; they send each other up with bawdy repartee. 'So who is getting Big Tits on Saturday night?' they ask a particularly flat-chested middle-aged woman. And everyone cackles with glee.

We are at the seventeenth-century *fattoria* Santa Cristina, and as far as the eye can see Antinori's beautifully-kept vineyards undulate. No wonder the family love to come riding through these lush, productive hills.

Such an idyllic spot is a far cry from Italian wine scandals, dangerous alcohol boosters used in an increasingly cut-throat market. People spend more, drink better these days. And naturally feel more confident in a name they know. But even prestigious and irreproachable wines like Antinori must undergo stricter export controls, with consequent delays in shipment. The situation is much worse for the hundreds of small producers, whose names are less well known but who make excellent wines. Around Radda, I have tasted them: Vigna Vecchia, Monte Vertine. The wine of an Englishman, John Dunkley, who dresses in medieval costume for the Chianti League ceremonies. And at Panzano, Castello dei Rampolla, with its landscaped swimming pool over the cellars, which provides water from sprinklers to cool the vats.

Tuscany survived the excesses of baroque and the last Medici. It will certainly survive Chernobyl and the odd wine scandal or two.

ALBERESE

Seggiano

SATURNIA

AREZZO

— PART IV —
HARVEST

PARADISE OF EXILES

FLORENCE

Dante would be deeply shocked, Shelley less so by the state of Le Cascine park today. Dante hankered for the good old days of Florence, 'abode aforetime, peaceful, temperate, chaste.' And here, Shelley wrote 'Ode To the West Wind' – as he says in his footnote – 'On a day when that tempestuous wind . . . was collecting the vapours which pour down the autumnal rains.' No poets nowadays roam its bosky acres; it is a paradise not of exiles but pick-ups.

Around 1820, when Shelley's inspiration in that park encouraged him to call Tuscany 'a paradise of exiles', a romantic Dantesque hankering for the Good Old Days unleashed the foreign invasion. Byron came, Keats came. Dostoevsky followed. And Trollope. And the Pre-Raphaelite artists Millais and Rossetti. Then the Americans – Mark Twain and Nathaniel Hawthorne. And people of no particular name or talent, but who prided themselves on being good humanists.

CASTELLINA IN CHIANTI

PENSIONE BENCISTA

Most foreigners, wedded to some mythic ideal of the Renaissance, read Ruskin and trudged the museums in reverent awe, their womenfolk blushing at so much nudity. But a few found, instead of a Harvest Festival at the English Church, a rich harvest of personal experience in the autumnal glow of that gold and red-roofed city, and its exotic sun-blessed hills. Botticelli was 'discovered' by the Victorians. So was Fiesole.

But I share Mary McCarthy's tetchiness with the twee folk who talked of Our Own Dear Florence. 'A false idea of Florence grew up in the nineteenth century, thanks in great part to the Brownings and their readers – a tool-leather idea of Florence as a dear bit of the old world. Old maids of both sexes – retired librarians, governesses, ladies with reduced incomes, gentlemen painters, gentlemen sculptors, gentlemen poets, anaemic amateurs and daubers of every kind – "fell in love" with Florence and settled down to make it home.' (*The Stones of Florence*)

That home might well have been the Pensione Bencistà at San Domenico. Even today, it has a totally Victorian atmosphere, within a gentle *carrozza* ride of the Fra Angelicos at the nearby monastery. There, at a side door we ring the bell for a private view. A heavy-breathing, rather grumpy caretaker puts on the lights; and there, in all their glory, are the *Cruxifixion* and some sketches of Virgin and Child in the very place the monk painted, 'in peace and freedom from anxiety', remote from pushy, sophisticated Florence.

Who could begrudge the Victorians such a treat? Or afterwards, that perfect plate of pasta off crisp white linen at the Bencistà, and a numbered metal tag to hang on one's wine bottle. Or the dog-eared copy of Vasari's *Lives of the Artists* in the *sala*, where an old man reads a *Daily Telegraph* three weeks old. Or terraced meadows falling away towards a distant vista of the Duomo. I remember with fondness great aunts with their Baedekers, the sort of

Pensione Bencista

English women from whom the Florentine film director, Franco Zeffirelli, learned English. I even have a room with a view.

'. . . the lights dancing in the Arno and the cypresses of San Miniato, and the foot-hills of the Apennines, black against the rising moon,' are Lucy's spring awakening in E.M. Forster's *A Room With A View*. Tuscany's sensuality and violence liberate this free-spirited young Edwardian from the straightjacket of upper-middle class morality. In Florence she falls madly in love with an unsuitable Englishman. Not our class, dear. But in the end she honeymoons with him in the very pensione where they first met. '. . . they heard the river, bearing down the snows of winter into the Mediterranean.'

In *Where Angels Fear To Tread*, E. M. Forster's other Tuscan novel, the English widow Lilia marries an unsuitable man, too – this time, a Tuscan. And worse still, Gino is a dentist. 'A dentist in fairyland!' bewails Lilia's brother, Philip, one of the Our-Own-Dear-Florence brigade. 'For three years he had sung the praises of Italians, but he had never contemplated having one for a relative.'

Others turn a more savage eye on foreigners in Tuscany. While satirizing the French nineteenth-century romantic novel, Anatole France in *The Red Lily* also spoofs the arty-craftiness of a fey Scots poetess, Miss Bell. Her poetry, naturally influenced by Dante, '. . . suggests an Italy veiled in the mists of the land of Thule'. Miss Bell arranges all sorts of treats for her French friends: '. . . I will teach you some fifteenth-century Tuscan dances, discovered in a manuscript by Mr Morison, the doyen of London librarians.'

My own favourite is William Dean Howells' *Indian Summer* (1886), an intimist tale of American Florentines. During the languid growth of love between Midwestern newspaperman Colville and Mrs Bowen, a widow, nothing much happens but a lot is learned. About the pecking order of High Society, for instance. Colville finds New Yorkers actually deigning to speak with Midwesterners at Mrs Bowen's soirées, yet Mrs Bowen herself '. . . was not, of course, asked to the great Princess Strozzi ball, where the Florentine nobility appeared in their medieval pomp – the veritable costumes – of their ancestors; only a rich American banking family went, and their distinction was spoken of under the breath; but any glory short of this was within Mrs Bowen's reach.'

Whether evoking Florence's rigorous winter, or the sentimentality of rococo statues, or a popular carnival ball, Howells is on a par with his friend Henry James for Italian spirit of place. And he can be much funnier: 'The Americans and the Etruscans are very much alike in that they always want to show you their tombs.'

Already by the turn of the century, Bernard Berenson

PONTE VECCHIO, FLORENCE

S. GUISTO ALLE MONACHE

All of this would seem like a typical American rags-to-riches story, were it not for Berenson's deep interior malaise. He felt his time was wasted on pedantic scholarship, that art expertise was not creative, that he was just another Victorian leech on the talent of the Renaissance. It is touching, therefore, to know that he found solace in the Tuscan countryside, walking in the woods above Fiesole, coming from the glare of hot piazzas into the cool of incense-smelling churches. There was one particular oak tree, ancient as an Etruscan wall; Berenson loved to touch it. It made him feel neither Jewish, nor Catholic, but pagan. He was at one with nature.

Meanwhile Italy was at one with itself. Soon after the *risorgimento*, the rebirth of nationalism under Garibaldi, Florence became capital of an Italy united for the first time. More than five centuries after Dante's death, his dream came true – even if this proud status of his home town only lasted from 1865 to 1871. During this time a strange love affair occurred between two exiles, a German Jew and a Frenchwoman.

In the climate of 1867, less anti-Semitic than under Cosimo III or during the later years of Mussolini, Jewish banker Sidney Hertz was created Conte di Frassineto by royal decree. He was the lover – or one of a cohort – of the wealthy French courtesan Fiorella Favard who, as ex-mistress of Napoleon III, had been exiled to Florence.

was showing Americans not tombs but picture galleries by day, and attending their salons by night. His 'conosching' (as he called art expertise) got the right collectors together with the right paintings – and so began the exit of Leonardos and Raphaels to London and New York.

Berenson needed security. For a poor Lithuanian Jew to become The Last Great Humanist of Western Europe, his own image of himself, needed *chutzpah* and money. His house at Settignano was an art mecca of society pilgrims. He became a Catholic. He married into the British upper class.

AVENA

ALBERESE

SPEDALETTO

'We were always told she was a great-aunt,' says the count's grand-daughter, Marinetta. 'But there's something dubious about aunts, don't you think? I think she was a mother. And her sins were hidden in a banker's home.' In other words the present Contessa di Frassineto is descended from an illegitimate child of Fiorella Favard – by Napoleon III. 'Well, that's my invention,' she tells us with a chuckle.

Contessa Marinetta di Frassineto, though well over eighty, still takes an active interest in breeding prize Chianina bulls at her Fontarronco ranch. 'Don't put agriculture in your book. It'll bore people stiff. Stick to art.'

She agrees, however, to show us one of the world's biggest bulls. 'I am bull-headed myself,' she insists as a gum-chewing young chauffeur helps her into the modest Alfa Romeo that will take us to the farm. 'I just want to live comfortably in the country. So I export semen to America. Bull's semen, you understand. So much cheaper than sending the actual bull.'

When I see the size of the bull, I tend to agree. The *fattore* is worried by our lateness at the farm. Have we tired the Principessa? Suddenly her title has been upgraded. From the farm-workers, it's Principessa this, Principessa that. 'Italians of all classes love titles,' she explains. 'I was once married to a Neapolitan prince for a short time.'

Carey gets as close as she dare to photograph the well-hung bull; there is something rather British about all this, like a photograph in *The Field* or *Country Life*. When I congratulate the Countess on her very expressive English, she reveals: 'Learned from nannies and governesses, d'you see. My mother was Verity Manners.'

Having given us her entire morning, she prepares to depart for a luncheon date. 'It could all be over when I get there. Or not start till two. You never know in Tuscany.' The old lady leads a busy life. 'I wish I didn't. I could be your great great grandmother – and still I have to work to

POMINO

FONTARRONCO

MONTE ARGENTARIO

eat. Honourable. But I don't want honour, I want peace – and that is quite another thing.'

Despite her great age, the vitality, humour and immediacy of Marinetta de Frassineto persist. Though descended from a French Emperor, two foreign exiles and a Welsh mother, no one could be more typically Tuscan.

Only the Tuscan nobility who still work their land seem to be effective. At least, they are the ones most in evidence.

Hotfoot from entertaining Prince Charles, winemaker Leonardo Frescobaldi races in his Lancia to give us lunch on his Nipozzano estate. For this occasion – different glasses for each wine, servants hovering – we have at least thrown a change of shoes into the car.

At 1800 feet, in the rolling hills north of the Arno valley, Leonardo explains that good wine isn't just the blending of grapes but the blending of families. 'In the last century,' he says, showing us a bottle of Nipozzano 1864 not even Carey could persuade him to open, 'we married into the Albizi family. Vittorio Degli Albizi was a great wine pioneer. His hermetically sealed Tuscan flask made it possible for us to send Chianti all over the world for the first time.'

Even as late as the last century the old nobility were selling farm produce from the back doors of their Florence *palazzi*. And Carey and I were told we would not get inside any grand house, unless the owners had something to sell, be it bulls, food, wine or the house itself. The non-working nobility are as hermetically sealed into their privacy as that nineteenth-century Chianti flask.

In spite of the informal charm of people like Leonardo Frescobaldi and Marinetta di Frassineto, the Tuscan character is not known for being sunny and outgoing like the Neapolitans'. They love polemic; as Stendhal said of the Accademia della Crusca, which protects the purity of the Italian language: 'They argue endlessly about language; they argue no less about the price of various oils.'

GARGONZA

The Italian Army had a battalion called The Wolves of Tuscany: Tuscans have a lean and hungry look, wild and alert; they are frugal eaters, eating only what's necessary to keep other wolves from the door. And themselves ready to take on the world.

We have also experienced the superb malicious irony of Florentines.

Dashing to meet a train at Florence station, in a moment of traveller's aberration I feed my neighbour's parking meter instead of my own. When I return, the traffic warden is giving me a ticket. I explain my mistake. 'I'm sorry – I'm just a stupid foreigner. Couldn't you tear up the ticket?' I plead. Comes the happy response: 'Tear it up? It is just *because* you are a stupid foreigner, you got it!' And off he goes, chuckling gleefully, leaving us with the ticket.

Nicknames are derisive, too. The manager of a Radda restaurant is known as *Pié Veloce* – Fleetfoot. He is the slowest manager in the business. Also, Tuscans do not like to see middle-aged men with younger girls. *Pié Veloce* clearly believes me to be just such a satyr, for he makes not even the slowest move with a menu. 'My daughter and I are starving!' I shout in desperation. 'Oh, your daughter, is she?' says *Pié Veloce*, still mightily suspicious, and shuffles reluctantly towards us.

Rude or polite, caustic or kind, it is wise to take Tuscans very much as one finds them. The trouble with the Victorian exiles is that they mostly failed to find them at all. Content with their right little, tight little expatriate cliques, the British of those Imperial days did not realize what similar characteristics to the Tuscans they had – introverted reserve, commercial energy, frugality, ability to survive long wet winters, and ironic humour. Both they and the Americans were content to bask in the attractive glow of Tuscany's past. Their idea of a modern Tuscan was entirely romantic and literary: a lazy, sunny, atavistic rogue who sang prettily. Those who met real Tuscans must have had quite a shock.

SPANDA, RADDA IN CHIANTI

RADDA IN CHIANTI

PANZANO

ASCIANO

FLORENCE

— PART V —
TASTING

THE RECENT YEARS

RADDA IN CHIANTI

A gentle blizzard of thistledown wafts across the lawn from the early summer fields, which already have a dried up look. It drifts beneath the parasols, landing on our hair and also in our Biondi-Santi Brunello di Montalcino 1978, described by an American wine writer in a state of ecstasy as leaving 'the palate stuttering' when young, and having 'a silky complexity' when fully matured.

The occasion is a fête champêtre given for such eminent members of the international Académie du Vin as Pedro Domecq, Ricardo Ricardi of Cinzano, Bruno Prats of Cos D'Estournel, British wine expert Steven Spurrier, and a cheerful, pretty American whose name tag reads 'Sylvia and her mom Doreen'. Our host is Franco Biondi-Santi, a winemaker with looks to match the smoothness of his product. The place: Il Greppo, the *fattoria* where

LE CRETE

PANZANO

Biondi-Santi ages his wine five years in cask before it reaches fat wallets and discriminating palates.

An air of leisured tranquillity and appreciation hangs over the whole proceedings. I am tasting Tuscany at its best. Here, now, not in a museum, not in a church, but in the southern Tuscan countryside where there are also simpler pleasures.

A smell of woodsmoke drifts over us. A pine tree grows out of a wall. Distant cypresses like a procession of tall, hooded penitents flank a hilly, winding road. The land, washed by an early morning rainstorm, is a patchwork of vivid greens and mustard yellow. And the Communist poster in the tiny village of Castelmuzio reads LET US FIGHT A WAR AGAINST FASCISM TO MAKE LASTING PEACE IN THE MEDITERRANEAN AND THE WORLD NOW! Somewhere a dog barks.

Peace at Siena, too. Another early morning feeling of well-being, even at the Hotel Jolly which is usually far from. I open the window, and lo and behold, floating from the Sports Arena is a green balloon, painted with poppies, sunflowers and a butterfly. Its surreal silhouette looks somehow medieval against the Duomo's backdrop, and now it bears its tourists silently drifting over the top of *Torre del Mangia*, carried on the breeze for a bird's-eye view of the craters and vineyards of Lorenzetti's country. The law and order of things seems natural, spontaneous

LE QUATTRO STRADE

RADICOFANI

today, needing no imposition of either good or bad government.

In the medieval village of Radicofani, the Tuscan Robin Hood, Ghino di Tacco, had the road from Rome to Florence pass over the hill via his castle, to take his toll from rich travellers. Suddenly the quiet town is filled with noise, and up that very hill comes the Mille Miglia. But it's a happy noise, and the whole village has turned out to cheer. Vintage racing cars roaring along the narrow main street, children waving green-and-red flags, an instant spirit of *festa*. Helmeted and goggled, the driver of a white

Bugatti waves. In a Bentley, a county Englishwoman is giving her co-driver tea from a thermos. Ferraris, Hispano-Suizas, the youngest car 1957. Vintage drivers, too: Arboreto and Stirling Moss. Competition takes a back seat; this is driving for the joy of it. And when the last car has passed and the knights of the road with it, we regret the silence.

My favourite celebrator of the Tuscan landscape, in the years when the Mille Miglia was in its infancy, is Osbert Sitwell. His eccentric father, Sir George, bought a half derelict castle called Montegufoni near San Gimignano, when his chauffeur took a wrong turn and broke down under its very walls. '. . . the drains can't be wrong, as there aren't any.' But its air of forlorn grandeur appealed to him.

Sir George's butler, Henry Moat, rustles up an indoor picnic of figs, *pecorino* cheese, and white truffles. 'And these things to eat and drink would be placed on a table covered with coarse white linen used by the *contadini*, under a ceiling painted with clouds and flying cupids, holding up in roseate air a coat of arms, a crown and a Cardinal's hat.' (*Great Morning*)

In the second spring of mid-October, the garden is a mass of plumbago, roses, carnations and lemon trees. Henry Moat recalls how a Balkan princess was caught stealing lemons in her stockings; and finds Sir George's

RADICOFANI

CETONA

instructions a bit mystifying, when all the staff but him are called Guido. 'Tell Guido to drive into Florence, fetch Guido back here to help Guido with the painting.' And Moat finds Sir George's retrogressive renovations tiresome, too. 'He has also pulled all the W.C.s down, and they are all down so no-one has anywhere to perch and the language is fearful.' (*Laughter In The Next Room*)

During World War II pictures worth $320,000,000 from the Uffizi and Pitti were hidden at Montegufoni, and the guardian Guido was paid seventeen lire a day. When a German general found them and ordered them to be burned, Guido blocked his path saying: 'These pictures belong not to one nation, but to the world.' And the general relented.

Tales of wartime courage abound – at all levels of society. Against SS brutality in the Casentino, against the savage Allied bombing of Grosseto. It is dangerously easy, surrounded by the unspoiled landscape of Tuscany, to bewail Grosseto's ugly high-rises, Poggibonsi's industrial architecture, and the characterless apartment blocks of Montevarchi. Tuscany was a terrible battlefield, and the new buildings one of the unfortunate priorities of peace.

At six-thirty fog patches on the autostrada clear to limpid sunshine as we arrive at Cetona, a sleepy, unimportant town with not much to see except the Convento di San Francesco. A market is setting up on the main square displaying salamis and cheeses, cotton dresses and jeans. And I think of Cetona at another time. Here it was that the town bells, celebrating the Allies' arrival, rang out too soon. Hearing them, the retreating German commander ordered his Tiger tanks to fire on the town, all but destroying it.

It was confusing for the Tuscan peasants. Whose side were they on? Suddenly the Germans were enemies, the Allies friends. The fall of Mussolini, whose agricultural policy had done much to stop the flight from the land, left them feeling betrayed and lost.

CETONA

In *War In Val d'Orcia* Anglo-American writer Iris Origo, married to a Tuscan landowner, gives a moving day-by-day account of action without heroics, compassion in the daily course of life. How peasants would risk everything to hide escaped prisoners of both sides; how the derring-do of the Partisans could be as dangerous as German reprisals; and how she herself, though accustomed to a literary, aristocratic life, moved sixty evacuee children from her house, which had been requisitioned by the Germans, to the safety of Montepulciano – a march of eight miles on a blazing June day, along a mined road, under gunfire.

The Prior of San Miniato preached a sermon praising the Christian faith of three young Italians shot by the Germans. Though over eighty, he took nothing back when arrested, and the Germans were forced to release him.

Not all Germans behaved like B-picture Nazis. The German Consul of Florence did much to alleviate suffering and protect the cultural heritage. Bernard Berenson, though Jewish, spent the entire war in Tuscany, looked after and hidden by Italian friends. The GI who liberated him is alleged to have said: 'What's a guy like you doing in a place like this?'

In Florence Santa Trinità bridge, which had been destroyed by the Germans, was rebuilt from Ammanati's

BOBOLI GARDENS, FLORENCE

original Renaissance plans. But according to Mary McCarthy, no one thought Ammanati, on the evidence of work like his Neptune, capable of architecting such a perfect triple curve. Academic detective work attributed it to Michelangelo. When the four statues were restored, the head of Prima Vera was missing, thought to have been looted by a black GI. 'Meanwhile all sorts of queer rumours persisted: the head had been seen in Harlem; it was buried in the Boboli Garden. The Florentine fantasy would not consent to the idea that it simply had been blown to pieces.' (*The Stones of Florence*)

BOBOLI GARDENS, FLORENCE

MONTEPULCIANO

RADICOFANI

And ever since, Santa Trinità bridge has been carrying the increasing post-war weight of mass tourism. Florence suffers its tourists as sourly as Paris, for it by no means depends on them. It became a boom town of Italy's post-war economic miracle, and still produces and sells the best: Gucci handbags and shoes, Pucci sportswear, Piccini jewellery, Loretta Caponi lingerie.

The high quality of Renaissance craftsmanship continues to this very day; we saw it happening in a San Frediano workshop.

From a modest alley off a suburban street, steps lead down to what seems to be the iron-barred gate of a bank vault. Top security. For behind it are the brothers Giorgio and Franco Salimbeni, and twelve craftsmen, producing expensive enamelled silverware. The Salimbeni brothers are bearded, Renaissance figures: Giorgio is in charge of production, Franco looks after the business.

Not surprisingly, business is booming. Art nouveau cigarette boxes, a photograph frame set in a blue butterfly, hand painting on ivory adorn their showcase. Some objects are flash and showy, just the thing for a jet set wedding; others discreet and Bond Street, more suitable for a silver wedding.

'Look at the work that goes into it! It's all in the finishing.' Giorgio talks with his hands, every phrase with its gesture of emphasis. In the basement workshop, enamellers and engravers of all ages work in a silence of dedicated concentration. A young girl has learned engine-turning. Giorgio shows us an old hand-operated machine which makes varying patterns on the artefact's metal. 'Very difficult to use,' he says proudly. 'This girl is a real craftsman before she's twenty!'

The collaborative enthusiasm of the workshop seems not much changed since Benvenuto Cellini was an apprentice goldsmith: '. . . and the divine Michelangelo . . . praised my work so highly that I began to burn with ambition to do really well.' The fierce individuality is still there, too. Salimbeni do special orders: for a rich Sicilian, a map of Sicily with just his town on it, a jewel inlaid in onyx; for an American, his favourite racehorse enamelled on a cigar-box.

It is said of Florence that you can get anything made there, if you're prepared to pay for it. The only thing you can't find is anywhere to park, while you're shopping.

Traffic is insane. Hit Florence in rush hour, and Florence hits you right back. Every time Florentines embark on helpful roadworks or underground car parks, they strike more cultural remains; only the other day a new Michelangelo was discovered. Meanwhile endless restoration goes on, as pollution does its worst to the existing frescoes.

One is tempted to ask: what's good about Florence these

FLORENCE

days, apart from its eternal glories? Well, there's the music, for instance. Mayor Massimo Bogianchino, former director of the Florence opera, has put Tuscany on the musical map.

In fact, it was never far off it. Cellini's organ-maker father wanted him to be a flute-player. A Frescobaldi – Girolamo – was a famous seventeenth-century organist and composer. Cosimo III's gay son Ferdinando had Scarlatti composing works for the theatre he built in Prato. The girls round Lake Massaciuccoli, where Lucca-born composer Puccini had his hunting lodge, are still called Tosca and Fedora after the heroines of his operas. William Walton and Edith Sitwell premiered 'Façade' at the Siena Festival.

Today, at Badia a Coltibuono, Paolo Stucchi-Prinetti, 29, makes cellos with

FLORENCE

six other luthiers. And at Gargonza, Teresa Guicciardini tells me: 'We have concerts for new works like Daniele Lombardi's "Poem for Sounds, Signs and Coloured Lights". Lasers and computers all over the castle.'

Tuscany's contemporary music for me is the bands of beautiful girls and boys, revving and weaving their Vespas in wild counterpoint, buzzing like demented bees through the city on Saturday night. Fatalistic and full of bravado, the girls let their black hair flow out behind them like modern Valkyries.

A boy, wearing loose-fitting Japanese trousers, whistles his dog, which jumps on to his Vespa, and away they go.

How confident they look, the gilded youth of Florence, off to eat and socialize at Acqua al 2 and Gorga. Everyone, I'm told, is into simple, fun restaurants which serve vegetables fresh from the market.

'That's where my crowd goes,' says 23-year-old Albiera Antinori, who gives good advice on how to enjoy the city. 'Don't try to do too much. I take visitors to just three favourite places: the dome of the Cathedral, where you can walk round inside and see Brunelleschi's work close to; and his churches of San Lorenzo and Santo Spirito.'

But Albiera by no means lives in the past. One day she hopes to run the family wine business – with her own

S. Lorenzo, Florence

BADIA A COLTIBUONO

hectares of vine and olives which have been in the family for three generations. Piero himself married Edda, daughter of a local *contadino*. The Mariottis, like the Antinoris, have no sons. So when their 21-year-old daughter Carla marries, will there be *divisione dei beni*, sharing of property? It depends. If Carla's future husband comes from the neighbourhood and has land of his own, fine. But an outsider? That could be tricky.

Carla doesn't seem unduly worried. And her younger sister, Elisabetta, is going to Milan to be a model. Very independent girls, they seem. 'I believe in equal rights for women,' says their father, rather to my surprise. 'As long as they help with the harvest!' adds Edda – with feeling.

Piero Mariotti's own independence manifests itself by cutting out the middleman and selling direct from his *cantina*. People bring demijohns and bottles to the cellar for a fill-up of red. Also for the excellent Mariotti *vin santo*.

Vin santo, that delicious golden dessert wine, is called holy because it is often used for the Sacrament at Mass, good and sweet and easy for the priest to digest. 'It is made by sharp changes of temperature from hot to cold,' Piero explains. 'You can even make it in a niche over the kitchen fire.' Edda offers us delicious almond *biscotti* which go with *vin santo* like parmesan with pasta.

Or like independence with Tuscans. Around 1960 ended the feudal system of *mezzadria*, in which big

ideas. Now she is starting at the bottom, and with no false modesty tells us: 'It is very delicate being an Antinori daughter, I must learn every step of the business and really know it. As an apprentice at our Umbrian property, I am in charge of vinegar-making.' The Antinoris have no sons, and who Albiera marries will be watched with keen interest by the wine fraternity.

At all levels of society, the marriage of a daughter can pose problems. Piero Mariotti owns Podere Malpensata (Bad Thought Farm) at Radda in Chianti, farming twelve

RAPOLANO TERME

NIPOZZANO

the landscape changed. Many younger farm workers went to Milan for better money in industry; at Radda, for instance, the population was reduced by half.

Here we are at Poggio Commisario, an abandoned fifteenth-century farm at Nippozano, where an old hunchback keeps a few rabbits and chickens. 'It used to be the garrison commander's house,' explains Leonardo, 'when Nipozzano was one of the fifty castles in Florence's defence ring. But with the end of *mezzadria* many of these old houses became deserted for the first time in five centuries.'

The saviours of many of these abandoned properties are, of course, second-home seekers from abroad and the Italian cities. The trouble is, many houses are very large, with no amenities, freezing in winter, and, like a demanding lover, in need of constant attention.

landowners provided land and agricultural tools for peasants in return for half the revenue from their crops. Sharecropping's unlamented end meant more independence for the small farmers who got up at four and farmed with oxen.

'Everyone benefited,' Leonardo Frescobaldi tells us. 'As winemakers, we had better control over quality, because we grew the grapes ourselves on our own land.' But

A most romantic house is Spanda, home of British couple Ursula Creagh and Iain Fraser. They are permanent residents, working in Florence during the week, she as translator, he as linguistics professor. 'We simply don't have time to do enough ourselves,' says Ursula, though her son and a friend are having a go at converting part of

PIENZA

VILLA RANCHETTI, FLORENCE

the house into a flat to let. 'I'd like to sell some of the land, but it's a protected area. As for the vines – we don't even mention them.'

The vines were understandably neglected. Vines are always a full-time operation, and people too often fantasize about their 'little vineyard in Tuscany' without appreciating its sheer hard work and hazards. The countryside is deceptive. The views open and close as the road winds up to the top of hills, along ridges, down into lush valleys of chestnut trees, oak, elm and acacia, a landscape constantly changing. Often it is marred by the sad patch of wasteland where an old peasant has given up; or, more

often, where a prosperous olive grove has been wiped out by the two killer frosts of 1985 and 1986. 'I lost ninety per cent of my olives,' Piero Mariotti tells me. So what will he replant with, I ask, sure that the answer will be almonds or sunflowers as it is in Provence. 'Olives,' he replies with typical Tuscan persistence.

On a more mundane note, Tuscan persistence is also required when making a country phone call. It's alright at Sigma, the Radda village shop, where I can call anywhere from in amongst the *pasta* and *olio* and household goods, and Signor 'Giovanni' tots up my units to Los Angeles with a vengeance. But the public phone boxes need *gettoni* – tokens you get from a distributor that never has any. In a bar, it's not so bad. Kindness itself comes from a *signorina* who, though naturally clean out of *gettoni*, has a clever waiter extract three from the phone box, and I keep feeding them again and again to the greedy beast, which continues to disgorge them till I've finished. The kindly *signorina*, I find out afterwards, is an American from Philadelphia.

The American presence is strong in Tuscany. A well-known wine writer, Burton Anderson, makes wine there. And the vast, American-owned winery of Villa Banfi is pure Napa Valley, all silvery vats and white-coated, black-bearded oenologists at high tech control panels.

Americans, British, Germans, Milanese . . . Tuscany

LE CRETE

is responding to its latest foreign invasion with a typical shrug of the shoulders. It is, after all, a much-needed injection of new blood rather than the shedding of blood in the wars of the past. And it takes a lot more than either to threaten Tuscany's independence. Its well-being, like its sunshine, is soaked up gratefully by the foreigners – artists, writers, farmers, dreamers, lovers and lushes who have made it their home. And many others, like us, lucky enough just to visit this radiant, strong country.

Carey and I, fatter for the hospitality – wines in abundance and all that *cucina povera* – feel impregnated by the Tuscan spirit. Now it is time to go.

One more autostrada back-up. Another dash down a Florence bus-lane and tangle with the one-way system. A final hassle with Avis as we hand in our beat-up Innocenti. At the station the *Partenza* board shows no train departures to anywhere; there's been a wildcat strike, but I am assured it is being settled. Time for a last proper coffee, a last pee in the spacious, functionalist marble hall of Firenze Terminale's loo.

Then the confined space of my Wagon-Lit reminds me of my sins of omission in this short book. What? No Petrarch? No Macchiavelli in exile, quaffing the wines of the Tavernetta Serristori? No Ghirlandaio or the leaning tower of Pisa? I have not described the Palio at Siena, nor

the Palio Motel on the road to Arezzo. But I make no apologies. This book and its images are only a taster, an encouragement to drink deeper of Tuscany's riches.

As the tatty old night train to Paris rumbles and clatters into doubtful action, we open our last bottle. It is an excellent ecological wine, which through its very purity will probably not travel beyond Prato, let alone the border. Its label reads: 'This wine has undergone no oenological treatment, no sulphurous additives.' Like Tuscany, it tastes extremely healthy. Flinty, fruity, with just the right touch of acidity.

POMINO

SARTEANO

ASCIANO

ALBERESE

PHOTOGRAPHER AND AUTHOR AT MARINA DI ALBERESE

ACKNOWLEDGEMENTS

Extracts were kindly reproduced from the following books:

The Stones Of Florence by Mary McCarthy by kind permission
of A. M. Heath and Co. Ltd and Heinemann Publishers (UK)
and Harcourt Brace Jovanovich Inc (US)

The Last Medici by Harold Acton by kind permission of
David Higham Associates

A Room With A View and *Where Angels Fear To Tread* by
E. M. Forster by kind permission of Edward Arnold Ltd (UK)
and Knopf Publishers (US)

Great Morning and *Laughter In The Next Room* by Osbert
Sitwell by kind permission of David Higham Associates

The Italian Painters Of The Renaissance by Bernard Berenson
by kind permission of Phaidon Publishers, Oxford (UK) and
Cornell University Press (US)